ECHOES

OF THE SECOND WORLD WAR

TRISH MARX

Macdonald Children's Books

Published by Macdonald Children's Books
Simon & Schuster International Group
Wolsey House, Wolsey Road
Hemel Hempstead, HP2 4SS

First published in Great Britain by
Macdonald Children's Books 1989

British Library Cataloguing in Publication Data
Marx, Patricia
  Echoes: the second World War.
  1. World War 2 – Biographies – Collections
  I. Title
  940.54'8

  ISBN 0-356-16754-2
  ISBN 0-356-16755-0 pbk

Printed in Great Britain by Mackays of
Chatham PLC, Letchworth

Contents

To Patrick, Molly and Annie, my
inspiration,
Owen, my motivation,
and those in this book, my education.

Foreword

I have interviewed seven people for this book, six of whom spent a good portion of their childhood, or late childhood, directly involved in the most devastating war this world has known. These children, due to circumstances beyond their control, found themselves in conditions of upheaval, deprivation and great uncertainty. All of them, at one time or another, mentioned how lucky they had been, and indeed they were, but they also had a determination to use their luck, and a clear realization that life involves choices.

By luck, by spirit and by conviction, these people are survivors, and they represent the part of all of us, the survivor part, that would emerge were we to find ourselves in similar situations.

I should like to thank: Focus Information Service; Allison Day; Richard Tames; The Japanese Embassy; Caroline de Navacelle; Fr. Jacques Coupet; Gladys Godley and Tibor Fülöpp.

Trish Marx, London, 1989

"War makes 'everything different', but human beings are not altered, only emphasized on facets which in peace are less easily noticeable."
Mass Observation 1940

Hans Levy

Oscar   Elsbeth   Hans

Hans Levy was born in 1928. His parents were
Jewish and they owned a grocery store in Gladbeck
in Germany, a town north-east of Dusseldorf.
Hans, his older sister Elsbeth, and his younger
brother Oskar enjoyed an untroubled life until
January 1933, when Adolf Hitler became
chancellor of Germany. One aspect of Hitler's
policy was to persecute Jews and so the Levy
family, like many other Jewish families, were forced
to move from place to place in an attempt to escape
Hitler's persecution.

Hitler attends a
Nazi Party rally in 1934.

Solomon Levy lit the Hanaka candles and looked across the table. Oskar, Hans and Elsbeth looked solemn, but their eyes were shining with excitement. They loved the Hanaka dinner, the best starched tablecloth, and the crystal wineglasses. Hans smiled at his mother as she ladled his soup into the delicate china bowl. Right then, he felt everything he needed or could want was in this room.

Yet only a few months later, when Hans was six years old, he returned from school to find a car parked outside the house, it was the SS or Secret Police.

The windows of his family's grocery store had been smashed, the shop ransacked and the words, "Don't buy from Jews" had been scrawled on the door.

During the period 1933–1939 there were many changes in Germany. Hitler declared his party the National Socialist Party, the only legal party. Racial laws were passed against Jews and other minority groups living in Germany.

A Nazi warning not to buy from Jewish owned shops.

9

The Levy family abandoned what was left of their shop and their home and fled to another town. This was just the first of many moves for the Levy family.

Hans' father took a job selling wines: **"My father travelled all over Germany selling wines. He went mainly to farmers, but, of course, never told anybody his real name as Levy is a very Jewish name. If they had found out he was Jewish he would never have made a living."**

As Hitler's policy of anti-semitism grew, life for the Levy's became more and more difficult. Hans could no longer go to the cinema or swim in the public swimming pool. He was often called a "dirty Jew".

"One day I went to the butcher to pick up some meat for my mother. A customer dropped something from her purse and, as a gentleman, I stopped to pick it up. I heard, 'Don't you touch that.' This is not just my story. Everybody tells these stories."

The Levys' landlord worked for the railway and he was threatened with losing his job if he continued renting to a Jewish family. The family was once again forced to move out of their home, and they moved to Herzberg.

One night Hans was almost asleep when he heard the crash of windows being shattered and doors being forced open. He heard his neighbours' shouting and one man cry out in agony. Hans wriggled deeper under his covers and pulled the pillow over his head, afraid to move, afraid almost to breathe. Then he heard his own windows break and his parents' footsteps from downstairs. Heavy feet were on the stairway and his bedroom door was flung open.

Anti-Jewish feeling reached frightening proportions on 9 November 1938 when there was a national demonstration which became extremely violent and resulted in what is known as Kristallnacht.

"The light went on and there stood this huge figure, in the all too familiar black SS uniform. I tried to shout for my parents, but in terror my vocal cords were completely blocked. I just slid under my blankets as this giant walked towards me. Probably realizing how young I was, he told me I was lucky and left."

Hans was terrified, but he knew the immediate danger was over. He had lived through Kristallnacht, or the night of broken glass.

Hans wondered about his gramophone, it was the only belonging he was allowed to take with him when his family moved house.

"The next morning we went downstairs to assess the damage. Every window on the ground floor had been broken, the

Hans Levy

A bedroom ransacked during Kristallnacht.

living room was an absolute shambles. The cupboards had been overturned and were lying on the floor containing now shatters of family heirlooms from a century ago. Chairs and settees were ripped open. But they had not touched my

precious gramophone, in a cabinet of
ebony. It still stood next to the overturned
cupboard."

Hans' mother and father thought
Kristallnacht had only occurred in their
town, and the next day they fled, with
Hans' uncle's family to a near-by town.
On the way, they saw synagogues and
Jewish homes burning and realized
Kristallnacht was an organized attack by
the Nazi government against all German
Jewish families . . . a warning to all
German-speaking Jews.

Shortly after Kristallnacht, Hans' father
was arrested and held in prison for one
month. When he returned home, Helene
and Solomon decided their children
should leave Germany, so in January
1939, Hans, Oskar and Elsbeth were put
on a train to Amsterdam, each with a
suitcase full of new clothes.

The family always believed they would
be reunited so their departure was joyful
and filled with future plans to meet in
Uruguay, where they had relatives. When
Hans, Oskar and Elsbeth reached Holland
they were given the injections needed for
South America, but they were delayed
from going because their parents were not
allowed to leave Germany.

The Second World War had now begun
and Hans, Oskar and Elsbeth stayed in
Holland for sixteen months:

*Germany invaded
Poland on 1 September
1939 and Britain and
France declared war on
Germany on 3
September 1939.*

Hans Levy

"The Dutch people were fantastic, they took us in and housed us in one of their holiday homes for orphans."

Occasionally they would receive a Red Cross letter from home. This was the only means of communication that Hans and thousands of other refugees and war victims had.

A Red Cross letter sent by Hans' parents to Hans and Oscar in 1941.

The Red Cross transported letters through neutral Switzerland.

```
Dear Boys

    Heard long time not from you.

Now await new address.  Travelling

in a few days.  We are well and in

good spirits.

Our kisses,

    Mother and Father.
```

In May 1940, the Germans invaded Holland. All the Jews living there were in danger of capture and deportation to concentration camps so Hans and Oskar made a last minute escape.

"There was a Jewish Refugee Committee in Holland. This was headed by a woman called Mrs Weismuller, and she was a fantastic person. She played cuckoo with [outwitted] the Germans and she got many people out of going to the concentration camps. She organized a coach and a driver and with 60 other children drove us to a seaport called Ijmuiden and she got us into a cargo boat . . . It took us five days to get to England . . . the first night we were shot at by the Germans, they tried to catch us.

The war Hitler fought at first was called a Blitzkreig or lightening war. It depended on using land and air forces to overrun countries by speed and surprise. By May 1940, Germany controlled Poland, Austria, France, Holland, Belgium, Denmark, Norway and Czechoslovakia.

Hans Levy

The captain of the ship could not make up his mind [whether] to take us to America or the Dutch East Indies, but eventually he decided on Liverpool . . . nobody knew we were coming, we just escaped. When we left Ijmuiden on the boat the Botegraten, we saw burning . . . the Germans had obviously bombed a part of the town. That very night Holland surrendered and we had got out on the very, very last boat."

Jewish refugees land at Harwich from Germany.

Elsbeth, on reaching Holland, had been sent to a hostel for girls outside Amsterdam. On the night Hans and Oskar escaped on the boat, she found her way into the burning city in search of her brothers.

"Luckily we had some relatives in Amsterdam, (not finding us) she lived there, but eventually they took all Jews living in Holland into concentration camps."

Elsbeth was sent to Theresienstadt in Czechoslovakia, where by chance she met her mother and father. They had been arrested and sent to Theresienstadt a short time after their children had fled to Holland.

"My sister told a story about my parents. When she met them in Theresienstadt . . . my mother was terribly ashamed of my father because he was in jail there. He had a job peeling potatoes in the kitchen and he stole a couple of potatoes. He was found out and he was in jail for two or three weeks and she was so ashamed of that."

Later, Elsbeth was sent to Auschwitz, a camp in Poland. She was one of the few still alive when the Allied forces liberated the camp at the end of the war in 1945.

Anne Frank, whose diaries were published in 1947, tells the story of the Jewish people in Amsterdam. She died in a concentration camp (Belsen) during the war.

Before the end of the war 6,000,000 people were put to death in the concentration camps.

Victory in Europe (VE Day) was declared on 8 May 1945.

17

Liberation day for prisoners at Dachau
Concentration camp, 12 May 1945.

Elsbeth went back to Holland and learned
that Hans and Oskar were in England.
She then wrote to them there. Hans
remembers:

> "I thought she was dead and, of course
> there was great joy. She was in

Amsterdam and we kept in touch all the time . . . of course, she told the story about our parents."

Hans' parents had also been sent to Auschwitz, but not at the same time as Elsbeth. Elsbeth learned later that as soon as they had arrived at the camp, in September 1942, they were sent to their death in the gas chambers.

Hans, now eighteen years old, had lived in England since he was thirteen. The Jewish Refugee Committee in Manchester housed the children when they first arrived in England and Hans and Oskar were so settled and happy in their new home they turned down a chance to be adopted, preferring to remain together. They went to school, learned English, and Hans continued to study the violin which he had started to play in Germany.

Hans, Oskar and Elsbeth were separated by war, but after the war they were able to stay in touch. Elsbeth helped to reunite other Jewish families who found themselves alone and in different parts of the world after the war. Her family now carry on her work as Elsbeth died in 1986.

Hans is married and still lives in England. Each September, on the anniversary of his parent's death, he lights a candle in the synagogue, and remembers Helene and Solomon Levy, who were brave enough to send their children away.

Andreé-Paule

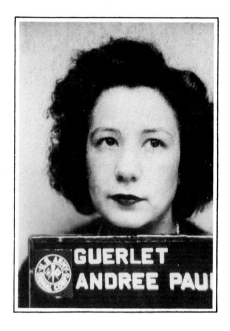

Andrée-Paule Mason was born in Normandy in Northern France. Her father was a diplomat so her family lived in many different countries. During the war Andrée-Paule lived in Hungary and Sweden and then was in Paris the day the city was liberated from the Germans. Andrée-Paule was 16 when the war started. Her age enabled her to make some decisions independent of her family. One of these was to join the French Resistance, an underground movement which fought against the German occupation of France.

Andrée-Paule Mason

General de Gaulle was the leader of the Free French, the French military movement which continued to fight the Germans after 1940. He organized the movement from London, where he fled to during the German advance into France in 1940.

Andrée-Paule loved to listen to her father talk. Because of his job with the French government he often had access to the most up-to-date information. She listened to his ideas on politics and world affairs and taking after her father, rarely kept her views to herself. The political atmosphere in France after the German occupation was very divided and Andrée-Paule took a keen interest in events.

"France was very divided and in many families some people fought de Gaulle and some people, like my father, were for de Gaulle. To know the history of France at that time, you have to understand how complex it was in the families – families would be very divided because they had different beliefs and different emotions . . . From the very beginning . . . my father never changed his ideas and I felt the same as he did. I was very eager when we went back to live in France to try to do something to help the Allies."

Many people in France were tired of war. The First World War (1914–1918) had destroyed many areas of Normandy and when the Second World War broke out the repairs on towns and villages had only just been completed.

When the armistice with the Germans was signed in 1940 many French people were relieved that they would not have to

continue fighting, but Andrée-Paule's
father was not happy.

"We were (posted) in Hungary at the time
of the armistice. The next thing we knew
Hungary was allied with the Germans . . .
We were . . . being spied upon by the
authorities and followed everywhere . . .
my father was always doing what he
could for the Allies . . .

We knew some Poles and Czechs and
they were trying to escape from Hungary.
We hid them in the Embassy and I
remember we tried to help them escape
from there, which was very difficult
because the Hungarian police were
watching the building. We had to put
them (the Poles and Czechs) in the boot of
the car and then free them when nobody
was looking. Hungary suffered very
much, but we left after the armistice
(between France and Germany)."

Andrée-Paule and her family travelled
to neutral Sweden. The family were
concerned about what was happening in
France but Andrée-Paule's father resumed
his duties as a diplomat, but this time for
the new Vichy government.

"Sweden was like another life, from a
comfort point of view. My father thought
it was interesting because everybody was
spying on everybody else . . . He heard a

*There was very little
food available in
Hungary and many
people were starving,
but the animals in the
zoo were not forgotten
and 9,000 straw
slippers and doormats
were donated by the
people of Budapest to
feed the hungry
hippopotamuses.*

*After the armistice
between Germany and
France, France was
divided into two zones.
The German occupied
area of northern
France including Paris,
and the unoccupied
southern area,
governed by the Vichy
Government, but
under German control.
The Vichy government
was headed by
Marshall Petain and
was based at the town
of Vichy.*

23

Andrée-Paule Mason

lot of information about what was going on all over the world . . . he sent all sorts of information to the French government . . . they were angry because he would tell the government that they shouldn't have accepted the armistice."

Germans occupy Paris.

Andrée-Paule's father soon realized the impossibility of working for a government he personally disagreed with. After only a few months in Sweden, he resigned from his post and the family moved to unoccupied France. Then in 1942 they moved to Paris.

In Paris, Andrée-Paule finished school and went to university. She was always aware of the tensions in France and now felt that she was old enough to help in some way. She read her father's articles for the Resistance and for the underground newspapers. She listened to his bold arguments, with friends and relatives, against Vichy France. She knew her brother had joined the Free French forces in north Africa. He had walked with an underground group across the torturous Pyrenees to neutral Spain. But in what ways could Andrée-Paule help? She was already working for the Red Cross:

"I was a volunteer and we had various jobs to do, mainly looking after children. Children were moved to safer places and we would pick them up at the train station and feed them and put them on a train to go south . . . If there had been a bombing we would go and help the people in trouble or who had been shot or whose house had been bombed. There was not much bombing (in Paris) but alarms went

Underground newspapers were published illegally and contained criticisms of the Vichy government.

Spain, although technically neutral, was sympathetic to Germany. Any Allied soldiers found within its borders were interned. Andrée-Paule's brother was jailed in Spain, set free and then sailed to North Africa.

25

Members of the Red Cross
at the Gare de l'Est in Paris.

out and everyone was supposed to go to
the cellar. But in lots of places in France,
especially in Normandy, all the towns
were devastated."

Shortly after Andrée-Paule's family moved to Paris she realized that with her youth as a disguise and her Red Cross work as a convenient excuse to travel freely around Paris, she would be useful to the Resistance, so decided to join them.

Working for the Resistance was very dangerous. Anyone caught in Resistance activities could be jailed, tortured, shot or sent to concentration camps, and usually their families were treated in the same way.

Working in small groups, called cells, the Resistance were nevertheless able to fight an effective underground war against German occupation.

Resistance sympathisers, hid members of the Allied forces in barns, sheds and backrooms, or anywhere else suitable as a hideout, until they could be escorted to safety.

Resistance workers inspect the wreck of a sabotaged train.

The Resistance also helped Allied airmen who had crashed in the French countryside, to safety. They would help them escape from France before the German troops tracked the airmen down.

Hundreds of bridges, railways and factories were blown up by the Resistance too and messengers, like Andrée-Paule were essential in passing vital information for all these underground activities.

"I wanted to do something, so I made several contact friends and I helped in two networks. Of course, nobody knew about it . . . For one network I had an invented name, because everybody had an invented name, but for the other I didn't. As I was still living with my family, I was always afraid that the Gestapo might come one day. I had to be very careful of this and, of course, I didn't tell anybody. I knew people around me who were deported (sent away) and who didn't come back."

The Gestapo were the Nazi secret police.

Only a few Resistance fighters were trained soldiers. Many like Andrée-Paule and her father, were civilians who found themselves involved in a war. They often had to depend for their lives on the ingenuity and quick thinking of others.

"I was very lucky. I had a pass for the Red Cross and so was able to go out after curfew. I had a special pass in case

something happened and I had to go and
help. Somebody once asked me whether I
could give them the pass, and they were
arrested. They swallowed the pass as it
had my name on it."

Andrée-Paule delivered her messages by
bicycle. Her contact person would give
her a message, she would type it, jump on
her bike and deliver it. Sometimes it
would be to a secret place where she
would need to give a code to enter, and
sometimes to another contact who would
pass the message on. Usually the
Resistance fighters knew only one or two
names of contact people, and often these
names were false.

Occasionally Andrée-Paule would
arrange an important meeting.

"Once I arranged a meeting to take place
in my brother's flat. These things were
rather risky but people were risking all
sorts of things. It was just a matter of
luck, you could have been arrested or
deported . . . or the entire family could
have been in danger . . . But I thought it
was terribly important and wanted to be
much more involved in the underground,
but I was too young to feel I could
completely break from my family . . . and
I felt a responsibility that if I did too much
my family would be in trouble. I had a lot
to be arrested for."

Andrée-Paule Mason

One day, as part of her Red Cross work, Andrée-Paule was sent to meet a train full of people who were being deported. Under the guard of German soldiers, she was allowed to give each one a drink of water. In desperation, the prisoners whispered telephone numbers in her ear and that night she called a few of their anxious relatives with their brief messages.

Most people rode bicycles as there were few other forms of transport. Petrol was scarce so there were few cars or buses.

"I remember riding on my bicycle for a weekend in Normandy, trying to get some food. That was a great thing, to go on an expedition to get food . . . Lots of young people went to see farmers to . . . get a few eggs or some butter and Jerusalem artichokes, which are a delicacy here in France, but we were just fed up with eating artichokes."

The Allies landed in Normandy in June 1944. Other Allied troops landed in Southern France and headed northwards to Paris. Reaching Paris, the Allies led by de Gaulle and the Free French entered and liberated the city from German occupation.

Food was scarce in France as in other wartorn countries, and Andrée-Paule could rarely choose what she wanted to eat. Once her family bought a large bag of grey macaroni through the black market and friends came by to take some for themselves. It was a treat for everyone to have something other than black bread.

Andrée-Paule and her family listened to the BBC for news of the war. Interspersed with war news would be announcements like the eggs are cooked', or 'the carrots are burning'. These were coded messages for the Resistance.

Finally on 25 August 1944, the Resistance was rewarded by the arrival of the Allied forces and the liberation of Paris from German occupation.

"We were so excited when we heard that General de Gaulle had come into Paris.

General de Gaulle's triumphant walk through Paris, 1944.

Andrée-Paule Mason

The southern part of Paris was already liberated and all the church bells were ringing. We were still not free because where we lived was near the Arc de Triomphe, which was close to the Majestic Hotel, and the hotel was one of the headquarters of the German army, so we were still under German occupation for part of the day. I remember looking out of my window and seeing the (Allied) soldiers attacking the hotel and there was some fighting. Then the Germans surrendered and the whole of Paris was

A German collaborator after debagging.

Andrée-Paule Mason

liberated. It was terribly exciting because one French soldier went up the Arc de Triomphe and hung out a huge French flag, and that was something . . . Then we all went to this big square and everybody was kissing . . . it was extraordinary. And then, at that time, all of a sudden people starting shooting . . . snipers!"

During Liberation Day it was dangerous to be out on the Paris streets. The German soldiers were nervous and pointed their guns at the windows where flags from many countries were now draped. The French who had collaborated, or taken the side of the Germans during the war, were afraid of being captured by the Resistance. They panicked and, in the chaos, fired their guns into the crowds.

German snipers open fire on the crowd as General de Gaulle approaches Notre Dame.

"I remember everyone lying down under the Allied tanks to avoid the shooting . . . Even when General de Gaulle arrived he walked from the Arc de Triomphe to Notre Dame along with his staff, there were a few snipers. I took my bicycle and with a cousin followed de Gaulle and several times we had to take shelter because of snipers."

After the excitement of Liberation Day had died down Andrée-Paule completed her education and became a volunteer for the American Red Cross and then a translator at the Nuremberg trials. She has since lived all over the world. When Andrée-Paule looks back at her Resistance work during the war, she says with conviction "I wasn't a great Resistance hero, far from it, but I wanted to do something and I did what I could."

The Trial of German Major War Criminals took place in Nuremberg, beginning in November 1945 and ending in October 1946.

Gladys Godley

Gladys Godley was born on 19 April 1934, in
Manchester. The Second World War broke out
when she was five years old. When she was six she
was evacuated for a year and a half to live with a
family in small town called Nelson, approximately
30 miles north west of Manchester. By sending
children away from the cities it was hoped they
would avoid the worst of the German bombing.
But Gladys was to be affected by war, and
post-war disruptions, until she was 16.

Gladys looked around the station platform. It was difficult to see anything, with only the moon for light, as the blackout meant that all outdoor lights were banned. Heavy black shades covered the windows of all the houses and shops, streetlights and even cigarettes were forbidden for the tiny glow of light they gave off.

The blackout regulations were introduced on 1 September 1939 and remained in force until 17 September 1944.

This was Britain during the Second World War. The German Luftwaffe (air force) was making regular bombing raids, but the British resolved not to give the Germans an easy target, even if it meant blackouts for months or even years.

Germany invaded Poland on 1 September 1939 and Britain, in defence of her ally, declared war on Germany on 3 September 1939.

What had started out to be an exciting day was now a tiring and confusing one for Gladys. She had kissed her mother goodbye in the morning and set out for school, only today she was carrying a small pillowcase in addition to her books and gas mask.

Between September 1940 and May 1941, the German airforce carried out a heavy bombing campaign on Britain, called the Blitz. 43,000 civilians, 30,000 of them in London, were killed.

"We all had a little cardboard box, and everyone was issued with a gas mask. It was made of smelly rubber with metal at the front, a gas attack was the one thing we feared the most. We found out afterwards it was useless, but we treasured it. This was our lifeline, that little box with a string around it, everybody walked round with them."

Labelled evacuees ready and waiting
with their gas masks and baggage.

Gladys's mother had decided that she
should be evacuated after a land mine had
fallen on her grandfather's street.

"Like several other houses on his street
Grandpa's house was split in half.
Grandpa was sleeping and when he woke
up his bed was hanging over the edge and
he was in it. My Aunt Minnie, sleeping on
the floor below and now covered with
mounds of plaster, was terrified he would
try to climb out of bed. 'Don't get out of
bed,' she yelled. Grandpa, slightly deaf

*When children were
evacuated in 1939
aerial bombardment
was expected
immediately. When
nothing happened
many children returned
to their homes only to
be re-evacuated in
1940 and at the time of
the VI (jet propelled
flying bomb) attacks
later in the war. Gladys
was evacuated in 1940.*

and disoriented, but otherwise unhurt, yelled back, 'What happened to your hair? It's all white!' And so it was, from the plaster dust. But they didn't care, they were so glad to be alive."

Gladys's sister, Elfrida, was not going with her. Though only sixteen, she was old enough to get a job as a riveter in a factory making the Bristol Beau fighter and the Halifax bomber.

This was no different from thousands of other teenagers who had their childhoods shortened when they had to take the place – in factories, offices and farms – of the men who were fighting in the war.

Gladys peered at the label tied on to her buttonhole. On it was her name and home address. She wished she knew where she was going. Even Gladys' parents did not know where she would be, but would have to wait for a letter to arrive from her telling them where she was.

The train shunted into the station with its lights off. Six hundred children, aged five to fourteen, and their chaperones, were loaded on. Each had been given some orange juice and two sandwiches to eat on the train. Gladys found a spot and snuggled down in a corner seat. The train started its engines and for what seemed hours, sped through the countryside. It was impossible to tell where they were

60% of children living in Manchester were evacuated.

During the first week of evacuation in 1940 4,000 special trains left from 72 stations in a mass effort to move the children quickly. In total there were nearly 3 million evacuees.

going because all the station signs had been removed for security reasons.

It seemed like an eternity to Gladys when she finally stepped out of the train at Nelson. Her pink hat was scratchy, her sandwiches had been eaten long ago, and her legs ached from sitting down too long. She wanted her warm home, her soft bed, and most of all, her mother. Instead, she was marched with a small group of children who were left standing on the platform, to a bus that took them to a church hall.

Children were assembling in halls all over the country, waiting to be 'chosen' by their new families, but this was small comfort to Gladys who felt very alone and frightened.

She sat down on the floor with her pillowcase with all her possessions in it, and waited. All the children were on one side of the room, and the people who had agreed to take them on, on the other side. They looked a bit suspicious, at first, of this sorry lot of tired, disorientated children . . .

The train routes were kept secret in order to protect the children from enemy attack. Everyone was warned by radio, posters etc. not to give any secrets away.

Snow White and the Seven Dwarfs was Walt Disney's first feature length cartoon. It was released in 1937 and was a world wide success. The dwarfs' hoods became very fashionable as headware for young girls and were known as pixie hoods.

"I looked a sight. I had black stockings on and my sister's clothes, they were a bit bigger than mine, but warm, and a pink pixie hood because the cartoon film Snow White had been the great thing and every child had one."

Gladys Godley

But soon people were stepping forward and inviting the children into their homes. "Would you like to come and play with my daughter? You could be a friend to Annabel."

Gladys looked up towards the voice. A lady and a girl about Gladys' age were standing over her. Gladys stood up, picked up her belongings and followed the lady out of the door, past the town centre ringed with shops, and to a small house down a quiet street. Annabel showed Gladys the bedroom they would share, and Gladys unpacked her bag.

Children arrive at their new home.

Gladys' experience of evacuation was relatively untraumatic compared to that of some children. Many returned home to risk the bombs rather than remain with their host families. Likewise many hosts found it difficult coping with the evacuees.

Gladys's first letter home complained, "We had some soup and they put too much pepper in it."

The government gave her foster mother three shillings a week for her care, and much of their food was rationed. Everyone was issued with a book of coupons, and this allowed them one egg, four ounces of meat, and one ounce of cheese each week, and one block of chocolate each month. Small children were given extra orange juice and milk.

A mobile information unit issuing ration books to families.

Because there were very few imports and because the production of home produced goods was disrupted, the government rationed many kinds of food.

The food rationed ranged from meat and butter to canned fruit and breakfast cereal. Soap, razor blades and petrol were also rationed. Potatoes were plentiful and were served in endless variations. Rationing was not consistent. The supply of food varied throughout the war so if a type of food or item was in short supply then it would be rationed.

With Annabel as her friend, Gladys started her new school. At first the local children did not like the evacuees, finding the way they dressed and talked strange, but they were gradually accepted. The war was quiet in the town – there were no bombings and everyone left their gas masks at home.

Other than the peppery soup, Gladys had few complaints. "When you are fourteen we will get a job for you in the mill," she was told. But Gladys stayed with her host family for only eighteen months, returning home to Manchester when her parents thought the worst of the bombing was over.

Some children were sent much further away than the British countryside. Over fifteen thousand were sent by ship to the United States, Canada, Australia, New Zealand and South Africa. Most children reached their destinations safely, but some were on ships attacked by German or Italian submarines.

The worst casualty was the City of Benares sailing for Canada from Liverpool on 13 September 1940. It was torpedoed and 260 of the 300 people on board lost their lives. After this disaster, the British government banned any further evacuation by ship, leaving the 200,000 children signed up to go abroad with few alternatives but to travel to the countryside.

Many children remained in the cities and for them the war was an immediate and everyday part of their lives. Oblivious to the dangers, they would roam the bombed streets and rejoice in the upheavals, excitement, irratic school hours and new hiding places created by the disorder and destruction. During the night, if there was a raid, they would sleep in the backyard in an Anderson shelter, a corrugated steel hut capable of withstanding anything but a direct hit.

If they did not have a shelter families would go to the nearest underground station and claim a spot on the platforms where they could lay their bedding and try to sleep. This was not easy with hundreds

The government had distributed 2¼ million Anderson shelters by the time the London Blitz started in 1940. They were sunk into the ground, covered with earth, had steel doors and could protect up to six people. A variety of shelters were used in the war, some people also used street shelters or Morrison shelters. Many didn't bother to shelter at all.

A family try out their Anderson shelter in the back garden, 1939.

Gladys Godley

Buildings destroyed by V2s
(long range supersonic
missiles), 1944.

of people tossing, talking, knitting and
jostling for a position.

Some families would queue for a bus or
pile in their cars every night and drive out
of the cities until they felt it was safe. They
would watch the bombing, sleep a little,
and in the morning drive back home,
ready to help clean up the damage or go
to work.

During 1941, there was a spate of
bombing over Manchester, just after
Gladys' return from Nelson.

"I was in an air raid shelter when suddenly the land went up and down, up and down, landmines were being dropped. All the lights in all the shops and houses were out and I went into our small backyard and picked up a large piece of shrapnel. I was quite thrilled. This was great. But we climbed out of the rubble to go to school. You still carried on going to school . . . also, at 3.00 pm every day the whole of Manchester and Stockport disappeared into the caves . . . sometimes

People in Manchester and Stockport laid planks of wood on the floors of near-by caves and used these as air-raid shelters.

45

Winston Churchill became PM in May 1940. He inspired the nation with his impassioned speeches.

In 1941 a utility scheme was started up restricting the use of raw materials for clothing and other domestic items such as furniture, toys and rubber products.

Clothes rationing was introduced in 1941. People were urged to 'Make do and Mend'.

it would be eighteen hours before we would hear the all-clear signal.

"Despite this, there was a marvellous spirit of friendliness. Everyone would turn their radio on and listen to Churchill saying the most incredible things. There was something about the timbre (sound) of his voice, the words he said. We were all willing to give 'blood, sweat and tears' because it seemed right. We were standing up for England."

After Gladys's return to Manchester, supplies of food became even scarcer.

"I would queue up (for food) before I went to school and when I came back from school. The word was out that there were bananas in Mr Jones' shop down the road. Queues stretched for blocks. We queued outside the butcher's shop. The butcher was all powerful as he stood there in his bloody apron. I did a lot of queuing up. And in school we knitted seamed stockings (for the soldiers) out of horrible thick waxed wool. My fingers were torn and the socks never looked nice."

There were shortages of cloth too:

"Clothes not only went round your family but they went all the way round your friends and relatives. You shared everything. You learned to make do."

The Government saved hundreds of yards of material by prohibiting pockets cuffs and long shirt tails on new clothing. They also tried to minimize the use of metal, rubber, plastic, wood and paper for anything other than making armaments, aeroplanes and for direct use by the forces. People were encouraged to keep and collect metal and paper for recycling and it was only at Christmas that any

Children piling up scrap after the launch of 'Be a dumper' campaign in 1940.

The German forces surrendered unconditionally to the allies on 8 May 1945. This is referred to as VE Day or Victory in Europe. The Japanese fought on for longer in the Pacific.

valuable resources could be used to make such luxuries as toys.

The war ended in 1945. There was cheering and dancing in every town and village and lights blazed all over the country. But the rationing continued for four to five years because there were still shortages of food and supplies.

Gladys grew up during a time of rationing and restrictions and when an opportunity came to be an airline hostess, she enthusiastically accepted the job. This was a chance to break away from the rather sheltered life she had grown up in and experience a more exciting and glamorous world. For many years she travelled, relishing in her new found freedom and education.

Gladys is married and has two sons and is a magistrate for the City of London. Not long ago, she had an opportunity to speak to a group of people in Nelson and she told them how she felt, as a six year old, coming to their town so long ago. When she reached the part about the pink pixie hat, someone in the audience spoke up, "Why, I remember you. You lived with my neighbour and her daughter. Welcome back to Nelson."

Inoo Foreman

Inoo Foreman was born on 10 January 1934, and adopted when she was one year old by the Reinhart family. Her adopted father was a (full time) soldier who had been wounded fighting for Germany in World War I (1914–1918), but recovered to fight again in World War II. He rose to the rank of general and fought in Russia, where he was later captured and imprisoned in Belgium.

Inoo and her mother had only each other to depend on during the war years.

On 22 June 1941 Germany invaded Russia, a former ally.

The Germans fought on two fronts – on the Eastern Front against Russia and countries to the east of Germany, and on the Western Front against Britain, France and countries to the west of Germany.

The Hitler Youth was an arm of Hitler's National Socialist Party. By law membership of the Hitler Youth was made compulsory.

Inoo watched her father's long face as he walked with a heavy step towards her. She was lifted up and given a gentle toss and a kiss. "Be good, liebling," he said. "I'll be far off in Russia, but you and your mother will be fine here in Berlin, and I'll be home soon. The war won't last long."

Inoo watched him walk out of the apartment building and into a waiting car. She had heard so much about Hitler and the 'blitzkrieg', that she almost believed she would see him again soon.

Inoo and her mother and father lived in a large flat near the Kurfurstemdam, Berlin's main shopping street. They were also close to Berlin Zoo and most days after school Inoo would visit the zoo or a nearby park with her father. She loved animals and she knew she would miss these outings whilst her father was away.

As the weeks passed, Inoo noticed how troubled her mother looked. She tried to cheer her up with stories she had heard from her friends about the Hitler Youth. Inoo was too young to join, but she tried to convince her mother to allow her to when she reached ten years old.

"My mother did not like the Hitler Youth. I wanted to go because the girls had beautiful brown skirts and lovely ties and white blouses. They sang beautiful songs around the camp fire and did lovely things outside. But I never realized about the

German children enjoying open air water sports.

politics, but my mother did know and she did not agree with that. Everybody had to go in and my mother was pestered by friends that I should go in, but my mother said 'no'."

Inoo could only listen to her friends' stories about the sporting activities and camping trips the members organized. Hitler had banned most other organized clubs for young people, and used the Hitler Youth to spread his ideas of racial superiority, declaring the blond, blue-eyed Aryan person superior to any other.

Because of a special agreement with the Vatican, Catholic youth organizations were allowed to continue.

Inoo's mother was disturbed by Hitler's ideas but was well aware of the dangers to anyone living in Germany who openly spoke out against him or the Nazi Party.

"My mother listened during the war to the BBC, which was not allowed, so if you were caught, you would be carted off, and if any of your friends would know that you were listening to it, they could give you away. Children who were in the Hitler Youth had given parents away, because that's what they were made to believe was right."

Hitler arrested and killed any German who openly opposed his party.

By the time Inoo was old enough to join the Hitler Youth, many of the organization's leaders had become soldiers, and many of the sports facilities and club houses had been bombed.

However, a generation of children had been trained to obey the authority of the government over the family and to remain loyal to the 'Fatherland' (Germany) above all else.

In spite of the war, life in Berlin continued as in peace-time. Plays, concerts and operas were performed and women still managed to have their hair done and bought new hats and clothes. Even oysters were sold.

A poster advertising a café in Berlin which sells oysters.

For those who were not Jewish, who contributed to the war effort and who did not speak against the Nazi party, the early years of the war in Berlin were almost peaceful.

Personal papers were important. People needed documents and certificates to prove who they were, where they lived, even why they were walking on the street.

Because Inoo was adopted, she had a certificate stating she was Ayran. Her mother was issued with identity papers and ration cards, allowing her to purchase food for herself and Inoo each week.

Jewish people living in Berlin were forced to go into hiding to avoid being arrested. They were not registered and were therefore not issued with ration cards, so this made it very difficult for Jewish families to buy food and they had to rely on sympathetic non-Jewish people to pass on supplies.

Work permits were issued to everybody, as were permits to buy clothing and postal identification cards were needed to collect mail. Documents were also needed to leave the city.

The first raid on Berlin was on 25 August 1940. There were sporadic raids until November 1943, after which a major bombing campaign on the city was launched. Inoo and her mother witnessed the destruction around them. They slept for safety in the cellar:

"We used to go into the cellar every night
to be safe from the bombs. You could
hear them whistling. Then, because the
bombing was very heavy and large parts
of the town were destroyed, we were
advised to go to the bunker every night (a
concrete building about ten minutes
away). You heard the siren going but, of
course, you did not have time to go to the
bunker. I was frightened in the cellar
because we also had gas masks on. We
could not breathe very well. We could
hear the bombs crash and you wondered
whether they had hit your house . . . it
was nearly every night. I remember our
street was burning on both sides – the
complete street was burning on both sides
– it was up in flames. I could see, up from
the top, furniture falling, crashing
down . . . Our house had been hit, but
luckily it wasn't burned out."

Berlin was almost flattened by the raids.
Before the war, Berlin had 25,000
streetlamps; 4,000 were left standing in
1945. There were burnt out buildings,
huge potholes in the streets and piles of
rubble everywhere.

"In the rubble (left after the bombing),
nightshade used to grow, and nettles and
weeds. We used to collect them and out of
the nightshade we made jam. It was bitter
because we couldn't get sugar. Only later

we found out it could cause blindness. We were very lucky."

Tram and railway lines were destroyed and riding a bicycle or walking became the only way to get about the city. Water mains were fractured and people had to carry buckets of water from street pumps back to their homes.

On 24 November 1943, there was a heavy bombing raid that damaged the cages at the zoo, so that many of the animals that Inoo had so enjoyed visiting, had to be shot.

It was clear to Inoo and her mother that they could not stay in Berlin any longer. With hundreds of other families, they moved out to outlying villages and farms.

"We took a lot of furniture away with us because we thought we might be safe

Unlike Britain, Germany did not organize mass evacuations for people living in large cities, but encouraged them to leave of their own accord.

Families leaving Berlin for the countryside.

there. It was a lovely time for me, very carefree because I loved the country, I loved nature, I loved to be with the farm animals. It was a large farm we were on and there were horses and cows and sheep. I loved to bring hay in and jump in the hay. But the Russians came nearer and nearer and we had to run away."

Throughout Germany people were opening up their homes to those who had fled the bombs, or lost their homes. Inoo and her mother travelled from farm to farm, leaving sometimes with their host family, when the Russians came too near.

"We had a lot of horses and wagons to put some of our belongings on; my teddy was very important to me. We got to another farm and the people let us stay there. It was a Shetland pony farm and there were the most beautiful Shetland ponies. They used to use them for

farming, they had little wagons. They would plough the fields and also take people for rides."

But Inoo and her mother were forced to flee again, the Germans retreated and the Russians advanced.

"The farm was in danger so we left our hosts and went further . . . I remember once we slept in the woods and that was very exciting . . . it was summertime so we didn't freeze. It was beautiful to listen to the birds. My mother was uncomfortable, she knew all the dangers ahead."

A few days later, Inoo was running along the road, ahead of her mother, when she suddenly felt herself being hurtled into the ditch.

"You could see the planes coming, enemy planes . . . and those in the wagons had to get out. My mother threw me into the ditch and threw herself on top of me. I was peeping out from underneath her and it was a plane going very, very close. That was quite frightening, because I saw a man inside shooting at the wagons and at us."

In addition to dangers on the road and not knowing whether the family would ever be reunited in Berlin, Inoo's mother had with her a huge amount of money which she hid in a purse under her clothes.

"She had to take out of the bank quite a lot of money. She did that early enough, then she had to see that she didn't get robbed. She had a little bag which she had around her neck and it went down to her tummy – she wore that under her clothes . . . later on we couldn't draw any money because the bank accounts were frozen."

Inoo and her mother carried on travelling across the countryside, buying food from farmers and fleeing from the Russian soldiers. For a time they travelled with another mother and her daughter. They eventually made their way back to the Shetland pony farm, but all the ponies had been killed by the Russians. A kindly farmer gave them two cows and a wagon, so they carried on with the cows until they became too difficult to feed.

"We left the cows at a farm and we just had a hand wagon, that you pull along. And then the Russians caught up with us. We were sleeping in barns, with lots of other people . . . some Russians came in, holding a torch and shining it on the people who lay there. They stopped in front of my mother. I was terrified but I

By 1 February 1945 the Russian forces were advancing across eastern Germany and were only a short distance from Berlin.

Inoo Foreman

A Russian soldier on horseback, supervises cattle that are being driven by a German POW through the bombed streets of Berlin.

prayed that no harm would come to my mother, and the soldier got up and walked away."

When Inoo and her mother heard that the war had ended they made their way back to Berlin. Once they reached Berlin they had to cross the east/west border, which was closed.

"We moved around trying to get back to our flat in West Berlin. That was very difficult . . . there was chaos in Germany. My mother managed to prove we had a flat and get a pass into West Berlin . . . we drove on a coal wagon on top of coals (the only transport available) and spent a night in a locomotive shed.

Also, to get across the border, she stuffed herself full of pillows to pretend she was pregnant, because then she would get better treatment. We did get safely into West Berlin and our flat was alright – but no furniture was there. Then the hard times really began."

At the end of the war, Russian troops occupied the eastern part of Berlin and the Allies occupied the western part. The border was difficult to cross.

A mother and daughter search for firewood amongst the rubble of a bombed house in Berlin.

Inoo Foreman

The war was over and Inoo and her mother were home, but they had no money left, no furniture or window panes in the flat, and very little food. They put boards over the windows and searched the streets for anything that could be used for firewood. Inoo's mother then found a way to support them. Some people still had Persian rugs, jewellery and other valuable items and the Allied soldiers

A notice demarcating the between the Russian border and US zones in occupied Berlin.

occupying West Berlin were very happy to buy them. Inoo's mother arranged for these items to be sold and received a small commission for each sale. They were still hungry, but at least were able to buy food and household goods on the black market. One day Inoo's mother was able to take her to the theatre.

"She had to queue up to get some tickets, and she was only able to get one ticket. She was behind a Russian officer and she said to the ticket seller, 'Can my child go in and I will sit out?' The Russian turned round and he said, 'You can have my ticket.' The Russians were very kind towards young children."

At last they heard news from Inoo's father. He was still alive and had sailed out of Russia on the last hospital ship. Inoo and her mother moved to the country to be with him. There they found lodgings in an old castle, by a lake, with several other families. Inoo made friends there and went to school.

When Inoo was nineteen she decided to live in England and train to become a nurse. Whilst training Inoo came across refugees with tattooed numbers on their arms. They were survivors of the concentration camps and Inoo was reminded of the horrors of Hitler's Germany.

As a form of identification, all concentration camp prisoners had a number tattooed on their arm.

Barbed wire being added to the Berlin wall in 1961.

The East Germans built a 20 foot wall in 1961 to separate the eastern and western sectors of Berlin. The people in the East are under a communist government, the people in West Berlin have their own independent democratic city government. Many have tried to escape from the East to the West, and have died in doing so, and crosses mark the spot on the wall where they fell. Yet others have succeeded, and look to the day when Berlin will be an undivided city.

Rupert Wilkinson

Rupert Wilkinson was born in 1936. His family moved to Manila in the Philippines in 1939 where his father managed the Theo H Davies & Co Sugar exporting company. He was also an agent for MI6, the British secret service agency. In 1941, when the war in the Pacific began between the allied forces and Japan, Rupert's father became the liaison officer between General Douglas MacArthur, Commander of the United States Army Forces Far East, and the British Government.

Rupert Wilkinson

The Philippines were part of the United States colonial power in the Pacific. There was US Navy and Military presence on the islands.

The Japanese wished to secure the Philippines for themselves as part of Japan's policy of empire building. They could then tap the Philippines' supply of raw materials.

Before Japan entered the Second World War, Rupert and his family lived a peaceful life in a comfortable but slightly ramshackle suburb of Manila. Rupert walked to school and made friends among both the expatriate and local community.

Towards the end of 1941 Rupert was walking with his family by a large plaza in Manila. The plaza was filled with soldiers marching, carrying weapons and waving flags. They were shouting "We are preparing for war to defend our country."

Rupert held his father's hand more tightly and they walked on. A few weeks later he heard a siren. Again, his father comforted him, saying "They are bombing far away in the hills, but the bombs won't hit us."

A street scene in Manila.

One day Rupert saw large sections of pipe in his garden. When he asked his mother what they were for, she told him the pipes would be buried in the ground and used as air raid shelters to protect them from bombs. Although Rupert was only five years old, he knew there was trouble brewing.

On 7 December 1941 Japan declared war against USA and British Commonwealth. By 10 December Japanese forces had landed in the Philippines. On 22 December they began to advance towards Manila.

"I realized war was coming. I remember seeing the River Passig burning. When Manila fell to the Japanese, the Americans had set fire to some enormous oil tanks. I didn't feel particularly afraid . . . I was too small to imagine ahead. I remember being fascinated because the oil spread on to the river and made the river look as though it was on fire."

The US and Filipino forces withdrew to Bataan Peninsular, whilst the Japanese began to bomb Manila which was declared an 'open' city.

The US-Filipino forces held out against the Japanese advance in the Bataan Peninsular but General MacArthur was ordered to leave the Philippines and sailed to Australia by boat. Rupert's father went with him.

With her husband gone, Rupert's mother was left to look after the family in occupied Manila. They would sometimes pack their bags and go and stay the night with friends and in return friends would come and stay with them. People from foreign countries living in the Philippines were ordered into internment camps for the duration of the war. Everyone had

Manila fell to the Japanese on 2 January 1942.

General MacArthur left the Philippines at the end of February 1942.

The US and Filipino forces held out at Baatan until 6 May 1942. The Japanese took 12,495 prisoners.

heard rumours of how bad the Japanese prisoner of war camps were, but they were unable to escape from Manila so all they could do was stick together for support and protection.

Rupert was playing on his swing in the backyard when the Japanese soldiers came for them.

"We were told to stay outside and play while they interrogated my mother. Mum told us Japanese soldiers liked children, so Mary June and I were not very afraid . . . we were just a little afraid . . . They looked tall to me in uniforms with peaked caps, and trousers tucked into boots . . . (they were) friendly, pushing us on the swings . . . Meanwhile the officer was interrogating my mother about what my father was doing, but they did not open the filing cabinet that might have held incriminating evidence about my father's activities."

Rupert, Mary June and their mother each packed a suitcase and were driven by the soldiers to Villamore Hall, a large community centre in the city. When they arrived, Japanese soldiers separated the men and boys from the women and girls. In the confusion Rupert and his mother thought this might be the last they would see of each other.

"We were all numbered off," said Rupert's mother. "The boys went with the men and that was the last I saw of Rupert. Things were going so fast. I got hold of one of my friends in the line and he said he would keep an eye on him. They all went downstairs and into trucks and we didn't know where they were going."

"I thought I was going to be taken away from her forever, remembers Rupert. "An older English boy, who I had always rather disliked, a bossy boy, was suddenly very nice to me and . . . he put his arm around me and said, 'Don't be frightened, we'll take care of you,' and that frightened me even more. I thought, 'I have to be taken care of!' I remember being separated for an hour, but I am told it was 24 hours."

The separation was temporary and when Rupert was reunited with his family, they were all driven to Santo Tomas University in Manila which had been turned temporarily into an internment camp.

Once there Rupert explored. The camp was a large walled-in campus with all the usual college buildings and facilities. At first everyone slept in classrooms, now lined wall-to-wall with beds. Boys eight and over were sent to sleep in the men's

Santo Tomas was the largest civilian internment camp in the Philippines, housing up to 4,000 people. Conditions were far worse in the Japanese prisoner-of-war camps for captured soldiers.

dormitory. The internees soon organized a Boy's Club as well as supervising the construction of wood and straw shanties, one for each family. Three to four thousand people were interned at Santo Tomas and 'shanty towns' soon sprang up all over the campus.

The shanty huts in the campus grounds of Santo Tomas.

At first, Rupert and Mary June spent their days together in their hut, but with very few books to read, no toys to play with and no swing, they soon turned on each other.

"We used to fight. I thought she was bossy and she thought I was a Mama's boy. I was faster but she was heavier and I used to tease her, annoy her, but as soon as Mum got to the hut I was as good as gold. We had an absolute tradition of not telling tales on each other, so she couldn't say anything."

After a few weeks, teachers who were interned started a school and Mary June and Rupert joined the other children for daily classes. They used whatever books, paper and pens they could find around the campus. It was a good idea, in theory, but the internee's biggest problem, hunger, soon made it impossible for the children to concentrate.

"We became too hungry after a time. Breakfast was a kind of mush with coconut milk. Lunch was a very thin black soup with sometimes a hardtack (dry biscuit). Supper was often a salty small dried fish, almost impossible to eat. This would be eked out with a small bit of corned beef from the comfort kits the Red Cross would send us."

The Red Cross worked throughout the war, all over the world. They delivered food, medicine and Red Cross letters wherever they could. These supplies did not always arrive.

Occasionally parcels from the Red Cross would arrive, containing canned corned beef, powdered milk, bars of dark chocolate and packets of cigarettes. Rupert's mother would trade her cigarettes for more canned meat, and she optimistically saved her last can for liberation day.

Rupert's mother remembers:

Currency was issued by the Japanese for use in the Philippines. This made the Filipino currency worthless and referred to as 'mickey mouse' money.

"Everyone had different theories of what was the best thing to eat. It was my theory that it was good not to have sugar, many people ate sugar to keep up their energy, but I didn't see what we needed energy for. Fat was the thing we wanted, and once in a while I could buy a tin of margarine with our 'mickey mouse' money, as we called it."

Keeping her children fed was Mrs Wilkinson's biggest worry, but to Rupert boredom was the worse problem. He read and re-read all his books and used every available bit of paper for drawing, mainly battle scenes and planes. He soon found a friend called Nick Balfour. Nick and Rupert would roam the camp, trying to stay out of the way of the older, tougher boys. If they met a Japanese officer, they had to bow their heads, but the most important thing was to understand the rules of the camp.

"The discipline was all or nothing. Basically the guards left us alone. But if you did something wrong, if you tried to escape, that was it, you would be killed . . . you would dig your own grave and then be shot. And if you received cans of food over the wall, that was also a capital offence. I only learned afterwards that, with great courage, a number of people we knew were secretly bringing food in by tunnel, under the wall. There was contact with people outside the wall, even though that was totally forbidden."

Mary June's drawing of a hut in the camp.

One day the Japanese officers lost a wild pig they were keeping. They asked the Boy's Club to help find it. Rupert and Nick were delighted to help, but another friend called Marian and her friends:

" . . . actually found the pig, and they became very angry because we got all the credit and the Japanese gave each of us a molassas sweet and a coloured T-shirt. We sat in front of Marian and her friends eating the candy and wearing our shirts. "

This plan was later used by the US government as a model for the attempted rescue of the hostages in Iran in 1980.

On 9 January 1945, US troops landed in the Lingayen Gulf, 172 km from Manila. They reached Santo Tomas camp 24 days later. The battles that followed for the liberation of the rest of the city almost destroyed Manila. The Japanese resistance ended on 4 March 1945.

Several people in the camp had radios, these were forbidden but it meant that news of the war filtered in. A second civilian internment camp, Los Baños, had been started in the hills outside Manila, and word reached Santo Tomas that the US forces had staged a daring paratroop rescue of the internees.

Speculation about if, and when, the Allied soldiers would rescue the Santo Tomas prisoners was increased when two US Airforce planes were spotted flying overhead.

Early in February 1945, gunfire was heard from over the walls. Unknown to the internees, 700 US troops had been storming their way through 60 miles of Japanese held territory to liberate Santo Tomas. After cutting through fields and fording rivers, they reached the gates of the campus.

The Sherman tanks crashed through the gates and cries of "They're here!" mixed with the grinding of the tanks as they slowly came up the main drive of the campus. Powerful flares outlined the muzzles of the guns on each tank.

One Japanese officer was killed and the remaining 65 Japanese guards fled to the first floor of the Education Building, a steel reinforced concrete structure used as their base on campus. The US troops, with all of their tanks, jeeps, water trucks and ambulances, pulled up to the building and began to open fire.

US troops marching towards Manila.

Mrs Meredith, a friend of Rupert's mother, ran through the crowd, her pyjamas flapping in the wind. "Do you realize our boys are in there?" she cried.

The Boy's Club slept on the second floor of the Education Building and Rupert and his friends were, by now, hiding under their beds and listening to the deafening roar of the gunfire.

"It sounded like a giant typewriter. I had a great tin trunk behind my bed, which I thought was wonderful protection. The Japanese gathered in the corridor behind us. One internee was killed by shrapnel or floor splinters. We were in siege for a long time (24 hours), but I remember thinking I would not be killed. Then there was a truce arranged and the Japanese were given safe conduct out of the camp. Under the truce, before they left, a great cauldron of hot corned beef stew came in, and it was delicious, we were so hungry . . . When we got out it was a small boy's paradise . . . There were soldiers, they were our guys."

When Rupert finally ran out of the Education Building, tanks, soldiers and guns filled the familiar campus grounds. The internees were celebrating their release whilst the US troops, exhausted, fell asleep in their tanks or under the nearest tree.

Except for a brief time away from the camp when his mother was ill with suspected tuberculosis, Rupert had been in Santo Tomas for two and a half years.

Young internees admire the guns of US troops after liberation from the Los Baños camp.

It took several months for Rupert and his family to find room on a ship, but by April 1945 they were sailing for California. Rupert's father was there to meet them.

A few months later, the Wilkinson's left California and returned to war-torn England.

"When we went home to Britain, I thought everything was grey and the cars looked old-fashioned (compared to the ones in the United States). My father was cross with me and said, 'Now look, these people have had a war.'"

Rupert's mother recollects:

"I had a new coat which we bought in New York and when I reached England it stood out because the people there had almost nothing."

After three years' absence, Rupert started school, finishing his education years later in the United States. He now lives in London and teaches American Studies at London University. He retains his sense of fun and tolerance that helped him through the years in internment.

"I have no animosity towards the Japanese," remarked Rupert's mother, and Rupert would say the same.

Toshi Marks

Lady Toshi Marks was born Toshiko Shimura on 23 March 1936, in Tokyo, Japan. She was the second of four children. When Toshi was very young the family moved to Niigata, in east Japan. Her father was a successful business man and they lived comfortably until 7 December 1941 when Japan declared war on the USA and the British Commonwealth, bombing Pearl Harbor, an important USA Pacific Fleet and air base in Hawaii.

Toshi Marks

"Toshi, Toshi, come back here," said her mother. Toshi stopped skipping.

"Oh, no," she thought, "she is going to tell me I forgot my bubble."

"Toshi, you forgot your bubble," scolded Mrs Shimura. "You must carry it everywhere."

Toshi walked back to the house and found her bubble in the six mat room, the large living area for the family. Her grandmother, who was sitting in the sunny eating area with Toshi's younger brother, gave her a smile as she walked out.

Toshi slung the white cotton padded hat over her back. All the children in Japan had been given a bubble, or padded hat, as protection against US bombing.

Lunch served in the traditional Japanese manner.

The war was beginning to annoy Toshi. She walked to her school in Niigata and thought about the bombing drills they practised daily.

"A bell would go off and we would all rush off to wherever we had decided to 'escape' to. We wore little cushions on our heads, bubble caps, to protect against things flying through the air. We also wore an ordinary cotton mask, it wouldn't help, it was a symbol.

We had to go to a shrine once a month to pray for victory; at six o'clock in the morning we had to go and bow and we hated it."

A padded hat.

At first Toshi did not pay much attention to the war. Except for her bubble cap and drills, life contained the same secure elements of home, family and friends that she had always known. She was only five years old when the war started, and she was still able to look forward to Sundays when the family would go to the park or a nice restaurant, and at New Year they would go on holiday. Toshi only thought about the war when changes began to creep into her routine.

Toshi noticed that every week, on every street, there was a neighbourhood celebration in honour of a young man going off to war. The night before the

During the 1930's Japan wished to expand its territories because of a trade embargo to reduce Japan's access to vital markets. Japan needed to find an alternative source for food, raw materials etc. Japan invaded central and coastal areas of China and was at war with China from 1937. When the USA restricted Japan's trade even further, Japan attacked Pearl Harbor.

81

Lucky bags being sewn by a group of waitresses. The bags were given to soldiers going off to fight and each stitch represented a prayer for the soldiers' safety.

soldier left, there would be a party and the next morning he would bow to each person, saying, "I am going now. Look after my family, I promise I will do well."

Toshi sometimes gave them a cloth on which she had sewn hundreds of red dots. The soldier would wear it under his shirt, as a protection against bullets.

"Of course it didn't work, but everybody had to do something for the war. It made us aware. We also had to save up every resource to give to the government,

cotton, paper, metal, everything had to go into the war. All our diamond rings went to the government, (the gold) to be melted (down). Everything had to be given away, the whole neighbourhood was watching."
"I also noticed the lamps being covered. And every night the neighbourhood watch would walk around the house and see if there was any light peeping outside. Everything had to be blackened by paper or paint. I hated the lights being blackened because I always liked reading books and at night everyone had to come in one room in the dark and you couldn't do anything. People shouted at you if a light was on. When I was sick I would stay in bed and put a little light on and try to read, but someone always shouted. I didn't understand why they were doing that. I was too young."

Japanese radio and newspapers were strictly censored. Only government announcements could be reported, and there was no international news.

In the final months of 1943, the Japanese began to spot US fighter planes flying overhead.

"When the bombing raids started in 1943(4), my parents decided to go back to my grandparents in their little village called Yamanashi, where there had been no bombing. My father and older brother

The first US B-29 superfortress raid on Japan was in June 1944. At first the US bombers concentrated on destroying aircraft factories and industrial areas. Later they stepped up their campaign and attacked Tokyo and other cities. They flew from bases in China and in the Marianas.

were called back to Tokyo to help in the war effort, and my grandmother, my mother, who was pregnant, myself and my younger brother went to Yamanashi. We went by train, it took us three days and we didn't receive our belongings for three weeks. Even now the region of Yamanashi is one of the poorest parts of Japan, so we knew it would be hard to survive there."

Yamanashi is a mountainous area east of Tokyo. The main food resource for the Japanese is rice and rice can only be grown on flat ground. Unable to grow rice on the steep slopes, the people of Yamanashi survived on corn, soy bean and a little wheat.

"It was my grandparents' village so we had some people willing to help us. But by 1943 food was strictly rationed. The first thing my mother did when she arrived was to plant. She had never done jobs like planting. Her cousin guided her, but it must have been very hard."

Toshi's mother was quickly recruited into the neighbourhood watch and she was away from home for many hours rationing out food and collecting materials for the war. Toshi, who was now seven years old, found herself responsible for the running of the house and the care of her younger brother, and later her baby sister.

"I had to look after the children and cook the meals for them and for grandmother. This was extraordinary for most people but not for us because by that time everybody was doing it. Had the war not broken out, we would have had maids, so we wouldn't have done that at all, but it wouldn't help to cry or moan because we had to survive, that was all."

In typical Japanese manner, Toshi would strap her baby sister to her back, take her younger brother by the hand, and set out for the day. Food had become very scarce and in the shop there were only a

Working on a farm.

85

few potatoes. Toshi did not like to think of food, everyone was hungry, and searching for something to eat or wood for the fire, took up the whole of the day.

Winter temperatures fell to −7°C. All heavy cotton and woollen clothing had been sent to the soldiers and Toshi and her brother had no socks, and only wooden sandles designed for warmer climates. They could take a bath once every ten days and even then had to share the water with many families. Because of the weather, bad diet and dirt, their skin cracked and bled, but hunger was still their biggest problem.

"I was so hungry I went to the neighbours and asked if I could help them. They were farmers and always had little jobs to do. They would give me food, some I would eat and some I would take home to my brother. I was sent to the black market for food because children could escape more easily from that place. I might trade some vegetables for two cups of rice. Meat we probably ate once a year. Soon we started eating ordinary grass, leaves, anything because we were so hungry. We would boil everything and make a thin gruel soup. We were literally bones, the whole nation was starving."

As there was no refrigeration to store the food from the garden, Toshi's family

Most countries affected by the war had a black market and Japan was no exception. Food and goods were available to anyone who could pay. It was illegal but it was a way of getting goods unobtainable with ration cards.

would boil everything, eat some and dry the rest for later. Toshi's mother had never grown vegetables before and they did not always do well. She was so proud of herself when she finally filled a small sack of sweet potatoes, but stored them in the wrong place and the potatoes turned rotten.

Occasionally sugar would be issued and Toshi's family put it in a special jar, but once, by mistake, someone mixed salt with the sugar. They could only laugh about it. "We called it the disaster area, but it was serious because we needed both the sugar and the salt."

Once a month, Toshi's father would visit them. He would tell them stories about the war.

"By the end of 1944, it was normal for him to see bombs everywhere. The person sitting next to him on the train was killed, or he walked half-way to Yamanashi without shoes because he had lost them in a bomb explosion, that kind of story. And by that time, most soldiers who had gone came back in a little box. When the soldiers were killed, the government gave a letter to the family, with a box with nothing in it. We were not supposed to open it, but just bury it. Boxes started to arrive everyday to someone in the village, so we all knew people were dying. And still we were told we were winning."

On 9 March 1945, more than 300 B-29 bombers flew over Tokyo dropping 2,000 tons of bombs. Strong winds created a firestorm which spread rapidly through the city killing 84,000 people. By the end of May 1945 50% of Tokyo had been destroyed and several million people had been evacuated.

One day Toshi's father came to the house and Toshi's mother stepped on to their front porch to greet him. "Yokohama died," he said. Toshi's mother stood still for a moment. In a way she was prepared for the death of her mother and younger brother. Because her brother was ill with consumption, he could not be evacuated, so Toshi's grandmother and uncle stayed in Yokohama, their home outside Tokyo, and both were killed in one of the worst bombing raids of the war.

Until now, Toshi had seen few aeroplanes, but by 1945 the war had come to Yamanashi.

"The Americans would come and 300 or more planes would fly over and bomb the town in the valley. The town was bombed for three days. It was quite big and there were ammunition factories there. Everything was black, completely dark all around. The town was burning for three days and nights."

Suddenly, in August 1945, Toshi's father was sent home from Tokyo, but he was not told why. Many of the people in Japan did not know that two major Japanese cities had been destroyed by two bombs. On 6 August 1945 an atomic bomb had been dropped on Hiroshima, a city on the south-west coast of Japan, killing 100,000 people and subjecting thousands more to radiation. A second atomic bomb was dropped on Nagasaki on 9 August 1945.

The emperor of Japan, Hirohito, was believed by the Japanese to be a god, but he had little political power. Nevertheless, he was able to convince the generals of the Japanese forces to surrender.

For the first time in Japan's history, the emperor made a|broadcast to the people.

Despite the emperor's plea, hundreds of Japanese citizens committed suicide rather than accept defeat.

"On the 15 August we were told we had to listen to the radio. We still didn't think that we were going to surrender. The Japanese never surrender, even in this situation, so we thought we were having a special announcement encouraging us to continue. By that time, of course, we had no ammunition. All we had was a piece of wood and we thought, we will fight with this piece of wood. At 2.00 pm the radio was on and we had never heard the emperor's voice before, he was god, but this funny voice came on and I didn't understand a word of it – he used very old, classic Japanese. My father said the war was ended. Surrender, at that time, meant torture, because the Japanese are told not to surrender, if you do, you have to commit suicide. The emperor said you must look to the future, which was telling us not to commit suicide, but to make a peaceful Japan. And after the war, WE DIDN'T HAVE THE BLACKOUT!"

A US soldier talking to
Japanese children.

*With the end of the
war came the
occupation of Japan by
US forces, designed to
stabilize the economy
and reorganize the
government along
democratic lines.*

At first Toshi was frightened of the US
soldiers who came to the village. They had
always been the enemy and Toshi thought
she would have to hide in the mountains.
But this feeling changed.

"They had a smile and gave us chocolate
and we realized the Americans didn't have
horns, didn't have monstrous faces . . .
But as children, we had more of a shock
than the adults, because until the
occupation we were told one thing, but
during occupation we were told a totally
different thing . . . that now we must
thank the British and Americans, that

they were lovely. For awhile we stopped believing anything."

Toshi and her family stayed in Yamanashi for five years, finally moving back to Tokyo after her grandmother died. Life returned to normal very slowly. Even when food was plentiful again, Toshi could not stop eating.

"Life was normal, but not normal. Children who felt starvation during the war had the craving (to eat) for a long time. Even when we had things, paper and pencils, we didn't want to use them, in case there would be another shortage. But the hard life came equally to everybody. Physically, mentally, we had to use every wisdom to survive. If it happens to you, it is an amazing experience. If you, as a child, have to take responsibility for your own existence, you become more aware of what you are doing. Children are amazingly strong . . . if they have to do the practical everyday things, they will."

When Toshi returned to Tokyo, it was hard for her to follow the traditional Japanese customs. She had survived a devastating war that had brought starvation, defeat and political upheaval to Japan. It had left four members of her family dead and her baby sister in poor health from malnutrition.

After the war, Japanese children used their old school books, but the offensive passages – by US standards – were blackened out. Often there would be only a few words left on a page.

Toshi Marks

A family in Yokohama having lunch. Their home has been destroyed by bombing.

Toshi was fifteen before she felt free from the constraints and effects of the war. She could not indulge in her passion for reading until she went to university to study politics and economics. In 1971 she moved to London where she lives and works as a lecturer and writer.

On 2 November 1988 Trish Marx held a
celebration party for the contributors to this
book. Trish had met them all before but this
was the first opportunity they had had to meet
each other.

Andreé-Paule   Hans   Inoo   Toshi   Rupert   Gladys

Trish Marx

When and Where

Hans
b. 1928

Kristallnacht

Hans, Oscar and Elsbeth leave for Holland.

Hans, and Oscar escape to Britain.

Andrée-Paule
b. 1923

Living in Hungary. Armistice in France.

Gladys
b. 1934

Is evacuated to Nelson.

Inoo
b. 1934

Inoo's father leaves to fight in Russia.

Bombing of Berlin begins.

Rupert
b. 1936

Rupert and family arrive in the Philippines.

Toshi
b. 1936

1941 ► 1942 ► 1943 ► 1944 ► 1945

Elsbeth released from Auschwitz.

Living in Sweden.

Moves to Paris.

Working for the Resistance.

France liberated from German occupation.

Returns to Manchester where heavy bombing.

VE Day.

Inoo and mother leave Berlin for the countryside.

Inoo and mother return to Berlin.

Japanese forces land in Philippines.

Rupert and family sent to Santo Tomas camp.

US troops release camp internees.

Japan bombs Pearl Harbor and declares war on USA.

Toshi and family flee to Yamanashi.

US bombing of Japan.

Atomic bombs on Hiroshima/ Nagasaki.

Illustration acknowledgements
Barnaby's Picture Library 10–11,
38–39
Bildarchiv Preussischer Kulturbesitz 12
Hulton Deutsch Collection 8, 9, 16, 37,
41, 43, 44–45, 47, 54–55, 56–57, 60,
61, 62, 77, 80, 94–95
Imperial War Museum 27, 32, 33, 70
International Society for Educational
Information Inc 86–87
Kurashi-No-Techno 81
Kurashi-No-Techno/The Asahi
Newspapers 85
Kurashi-No-Techno/The Mainichi
Newspapers 88–89
Laura Wilkinson 73
Macdonald/Aldus Archive 28–29, 31
Macdonald Children's Books 7, 14, 21,
35, 49, 65, 79
Popperfoto 18–19, 24, 26, 40, 51, 58,
59, 64, 66, 68–69, 82, 90, 92
QFT Photography Ltd 93
Robert Hunt Library 75
Topham Picture Library 22–23
Ullstein Bilderdienst 53

Subject Consultant Angela Godwin
Book Editor Lucy Ormrod
Picture Research Donna Thynne
Design Pat Brennan
Production Rosemary Bishop